Editor's Comment

A New LNG Hub in Africa on the Horizon

The recent large offshore natural gas discoveries in Africa have focused the attention of the international oil and gas industry on large LNG export projects that are essential to monetize these resources.

BP's entry into Mauritania and Senegal with Kosmos Energy as partner and the New Gas Discoveries in Mozambique and Tanzania points to Africa as an emerging major natural gas player. Even as, BP chief executive officer Bob Dudley said, "We believe our expertise in integrating the gas value chain, together with a talented exploration partner in Kosmos, along with the support of the Mauritanian and Senegalese governments brings together all the elements needed to create a new LNG hub in Africa."

In the meantime, OPEC has decided to play its traditional role of stabilizing the world oil price- is it a Trump effect or the animosity against US shale is over? Take a poll on our website to share your thought.

Still in this New Year edition- API **Recommended Practices for the First Time, Imposes Minimum Requirements on pipeline operators**- just as PHMSA issues Interim Final Regulations on Underground Natural Gas Storage.

Strategic Petroleum Reserve Sales Totaling Nearly 190 Million Barrels to Start in January 2017 Thru 2025. You will also see- Shale natural gas proved reserves, reserves changes, and production.

Finally-The largest infrastructure conference for Upstream, Midstream and Downstream– **International Pipeline, Oil and Gas Safety Conference POGS will take place in Houston Texas –March 14-16, 2017.** Visit the event site for more details- www.oilandgassafetyconference.

- Gloria Towolawi

Contents

USA Oil and Gas Monitor
A RGT Media Communications Corp.

Editor-in-Chief
Gloria Towolawi

Europe Bureau
Esther Coker

Nigeria Bureau
David Arhavbarien

Contributing Editor
Gloria Instead

Reporter
Caleb Motinwo

Advert & Marketing
Jewel Spring
T: 832-486-0095
E: advert@usaoilandgasmonitor.com

Distribution & sales
Richard Godfirst

Subscribers Service
E: subscribe@usaoilandgasmonitor.com

RGT Media Communications Corp.
Publishers of
USA Oil and Gas Monitor
Workplace Weekly News
GlobalPRPlus

USA Oil and Gas Monitor is published 12 times a year monthly by RGT Media Communications Corp. 10777 Westheimer #1100

Houston, Texas 77042
Subscription price is $144 per year.
Digital copy $9.99 per download.

CO2 Emissions from U.S. Consumption of Energy, totaled 3,876 Million Metric Tons In 2016- Petroleum Accounted For 45 Percent

Carbon Dioxide Emissions from Energy Consumption by Source
(Million Metric Tons of Carbon Dioxide)

	Coal	Natural Gas	Aviation Gasoline	Distillate Fuel Oil	Jet Fuel	Kero-sene	LPG	Lubri-cants	Motor Gasoline	Petroleum Coke	Residual Fuel Oil	Other	Total	Total
2016-January	125	168	(s)	49	18	(s)	9	1	90	6	5	10	189	483
February	103	144	(s)	48	18	(s)	8	1	90	6	3	11	185	433
March	83	128	(s)	51	19	(s)	7	1	98	7	6	9	198	409
April	81	113	(s)	48	19	(s)	6	1	93	5	7	9	188	383
May	92	107	(s)	48	19	(s)	6	1	98	5	5	9	192	391
June	126	109	(s)	48	21	(s)	5	1	97	4	6	9	192	427
July	146	119	(s)	46	21	(s)	6	1	100	6	7	9	196	461
August	145	120	(s)	50	21	(s)	6	1	100	8	5	11	202	468
September	124	106	(s)	49	20	(s)	7	1	96	5	4	10	191	421
9-month Total	1024	1112	1	436	176	1	61	8	862	53	48	86	1731	3,876

Notes:

Data are estimates for carbon dioxide emissions from energy consumption, including the nonfuel use of fossil fuels

Data exclude emissions from biomass energy consumption. Excludes emissions from biomass energy consumption. R=Revised. (s)=Less than 0.5 million metric tons. Geographic coverage is the 50 states and the District of Columbia.

Carbon Dioxide Emissions from Energy Consumption by Source 2016 9-month total

Carbon dioxide CO2 emissions from U.S. consumption of energy, excluding biomass, totaled 3,876 million metric tons. Of that total, petroleum accounted for 45 percent, coal for 29 percent, and natural gas for 25 percent.

2016 CO2 Emission	Coal	Natural Gas	Petroleum	Aggregate Total
January	125	168	189	483
February	103	144	185	433
March	83	128	198	409
April	81	113	188	383
May	92	107	192	391
June	126	109	192	427
July	146	119	196	461
August	145	120	202	468
September	124	106	191	421
Total	**1024**	**1112**	**1731**	**3,876**

Carbon Dioxide Emissions from Energy Consumption: Transportation Sector

	Coal	Natural Gas	Aviation Gasoline	Distillate Fuel Oil	Jet Fuel	LPG	Lubricants	Motor Gasoline	Residual Fuel Oil	TOTAL	RETAIL ELECTRICITY	Total
2016-January	(h)	4	(s)	32	18	(s)	(s)	89	4	144	(s)	149
February	(h)	4	(s)	31	18	(s)	(s)	88	2	140	(s)	144
March	(h)	3	(s)	36	19	(s)	(s)	96	5	157	(s)	161
April	(h)	3	(s)	35	19	(s)	(s)	91	6	153	(s)	156
May	(h)	3	(s)	37	19	(s)	(s)	97	4	158	(s)	161
June	(h)	3	(s)	37	21	(s)	(s)	96	5	160	(s)	163
July	(h)	3	(s)	38	21	(s)	(s)	98	6	164	(s)	167
August	(h)	3	(s)	20	21	(s)	(s)	98	4	164	(s)	168
September	(h)	3	(s)	37	20	(s)	(s)	94	4	155	(s)	158
9-month Total	(h)	29	1	323	176	2	4	847	41	1395	3	1427

Note: h- Beginning in 1978, the small amounts of coal consumed for transportation are reported as industrial sector consumption.

Carbon Dioxide Emissions from Energy Consumption Transportation Sector 2016 9-month total

The transportation sector accounted for 38 percent of total CO2 emissions from energy consumption, with 98 percent of the sector's emissions attributable to petroleum and 2 percent attributable to natural gas.

2016 CO2 Emission	Coal	Natural Gas	Petroleum	Aggregate Total
January	(h)	4	144	149
February	(h)	4	140	144
March	(h)	3	157	161
April	(h)	3	153	156
May	(h)	3	158	161
June	(h)	3	160	163
July	(h)	3	164	167
August	(h)	3	164	168
September	(h)	3	155	158
Total	**(h)**	**29**	**1395**	**1427**

January 2017 • Issue 1

Carbon Dioxide Emissions from Energy Consumption: Industrial Sector
(Million Metric Tons of Carbon Dioxide)

	Coal	Coal coke Net Imports	Natural Gas	Distillate Fuel Oil	Kero-sene	LPG	Lubri-cants	Motor Gasoline	Petro-leum Coke	Residual Fuel Oil	Other	Total	Retail Elec-tricity	Total
2016-January	11	(s)	45	7	(s)	5	(s)	1	6	(s)	10	29	38	122
February	11	(s)	42	7	(s)	4	(s)	1	5	(s)	11	30	33	115
March	10	(s)	42	8	(s)	4	1	1	6	(s)	9	28	31	111
April	9	(s)	39	6	(s)	3	(s)	1	4	(s)	9	24	32	105
May	9	(s)	39	6	(s)	3	(s)	1	4	(s)	9	23	36	107
June	10	(s)	38	6	(s)	2	1	1	3	(s)	9	23	42	113
July	10	(s)	39	4	(s)	3	(s)	1	5	(s)	9	22	46	117
August	11	(s)	40	7	(s)	3	(s)	1	7	(s)	11	29	46	125
September	10	(s)	39	7	(s)	3	(s)	1	4	(s)	10	27	40	115
9-month Total	90	-1	363	58	(s)	30	4	11	44	2	86	235	345	1,032

Note: Emissions from energy consumption, for electricity and a small amount of useful thermal output, in the electric power sector are allocated to the end-use sectors in proportion to each sector's share of total electricity retail sales. (s)=Less than 0.5 million metric tons and greater than -0.5 million metric tons.

Carbon Dioxide Emissions from Energy Consumption: Industrial Sector

The industrial sector accounted for 27 percent of total CO2 emissions, **with 35 percent of the sector's emissions attributable to natural gas and 33 percent attributable to retail electricity, 23 percent attributable to petroleum and 9 percent attributable to coal.**

2016 CO2 Emission	Coal	Natural Gas	Petroleum	Retail Electricity	Aggregate Total
January	11	45	29	38	122
February	11	42	30	33	115
March	10	42	28	31	111
April	9	39	24	32	105
May	9	39	23	36	107
June	10	38	23	42	113
July	10	39	22	46	117
August	11	40	29	46	125
September	10	39	27	40	115
Total	90	363	235	345	1,032

PHMSA Interim Final Regulations on Underground Natural Gas Storage

API RP For the First Time, Imposes Minimum Requirements

PHMSA has issued interim regulations regarding underground natural gas storage, incorporating API Recommended Practices 1170 and 1171. *The API RP would, for the first time, impose minimum requirements for operators to assess the operational safety of their storage facilities, and document the implementation of identified safety solutions.*

The U.S. Department of Transportation's DOT Pipeline and Hazardous Materials Safety Administration PHMSA interim final rule IFR revises the Federal pipeline safety regulations to address safety issues related to downhole facilities, including well integrity, wellbore tubing, and casing. This first step in addressing critical safety issues is responsive of Section 12 of the PIPES Act requiring PHMSA to enact minimum federal safety standards for underground natural gas storage facilities and addresses the concerns of the public highlighted by the Aliso Canyon natural gas leak incident of 2015. The Aliso Canyon incident resulted in the estimated release of 4.62 billion cubic feet of natural gas, or the greenhouse gas emission equivalent of 500,000 passenger cars driven for 1 year.

"Less than one year after the formation of the DOT/DOE Interagency Task Force on Natural Gas Storage Safety, we have developed an interim final rule that puts critical safety standards in place for underground storage facilities across the country and establishes a consistent, minimum federal baseline for states to develop their own regulations," said Transportation Secretary Anthony Foxx.

Following the nation's largest ever natural gas storage leak at SoCalGas's Aliso Canyon facility. the Obama Administration convened a new Interagency Task Force on Natural Gas Storage Safety. The Task Force pursued three primary areas of study: integrity of wells at underground gas storage facilities, public health and environmental effects from a natural gas leak like the one at the Aliso Canyon underground gas storage facility, and energy reliability concerns in the case of future natural gas leaks. It held three public stakeholder workshops to hear from stakeholders and the public, and produced a report titled Ensuring Safe and Reliable Underground Natural Gas Storage. The report contains 44 specific recommendations.

A summary of those recommendations is below:

WELL INTEGRITY

While the State of California is still analyzing the root cause of the Aliso Canyon leak, well records indicate that the leaking well was operated with a single point of failure design – allowing gas to flow through both production tubing and well-casing, making the system dependent on a single barrier to contain the gas. The Task Force's report found that if a second barrier had been in place, the

January 2017 • Issue 1

uncontrolled leak could likely have been avoided. Additionally, the report notes that the inspection program, monitoring, and risk management plan for this well appear to have been inadequate to ensure safety. For example, well logs indicate that the majority of wells at the facility had not been recently evaluated for integrity.

Based on these findings and more, the report makes the following key recommendations addressing well integrity issues:

New wells should be designed so that a single point of failure cannot lead to leakage and uncontrolled flow, and except under limited circumstances, natural gas storage operators should phase out single point-of-failure wells.

Operators should adopt risk management plans that include a rigorous monitoring program, well integrity evaluation, leakage surveys, mechanical integrity tests and conservative assessment intervals.

DOE and DOT should conduct a specific and thorough joint study of subsurface safety valves.

HEALTH AND ENVIRONMENT

The report notes that, following the Aliso Canyon leak, residents of nearby neighborhoods experienced health symptoms consistent with exposures to odorants added to the natural gas, thousands of households were displaced, and approximately 90,000 metric tons of methane – a powerful greenhouse gas – was released from the well.

To prevent and mitigate similar health and environmental impacts in the event of future leaks, the report's recommendations include:

In the event of a natural gas leak large enough to require multiple jurisdictions in the response effort, a "unified command" should be formed early so that leaders from each primary response agency can provide clear and consistent communications between agencies and with the public about progress toward controlling the leak and understanding the potential public health impacts of the release.

States and local monitoring agencies should consider establishing an emergency air monitoring plan that can be expeditiously deployed in the event of a leak.

States should review their authority to require

greenhouse gas mitigation plans in the event of a leak.

ENERGY RELIABILITY

The loss of the Aliso Canyon facility increased the likelihood of regional electric generation shortages in southern California this year. While communities were able to avoid electric curtailments this summer, maintaining electric reliability without Aliso Canyon remains a concern heading into winter. Other communities around the country could face similar concerns in the event of a leak in their region. Indeed, if such a leak led to a prolonged gas storage facility outage, the report finds that 12 of the nation's underground gas storage facilities appear to have the potential to affect 2 gigawatts or more of available electric generation capacity.

The report makes the following key recommendations regarding reliability concerns:

Industry, Federal and state agencies should strengthen planning and coordination efforts to decrease the potential impacts of future prolonged disruptions of natural gas infrastructure.

Industry, Federal and state agencies should consider broader application of back-up strategies to reduce reliability risks associated with the abrupt loss of natural gas supplies.

The IFR incorporates the American Petroleum Institute's recommended practices 1170 and 1171 by reference into the pipeline safety regulations 49 C.F.R. Part 192. Recommended practices 1170 and 1171 outline standards for the design and operation of solution-mined salt caverns used for natural gas storage, and functional integrity of natural gas storage in depleted hydrocarbon reservoirs and aquifer reservoirs. The incorporation of these RPs will provide PHMSA and the states with a minimum federal standard for inspection, enforcement, and training through a federal/state partnership and certification process modeled after the current pipeline safety program. The standards will directly apply to approximately 200 interstate facilities, and serve as the minimum federal standard for approximately 200 intrastate facilities.

"This IFR addresses aging infrastructure and is the first step in a multiphase process to enhance the safety of underground natural gas storage," said PHMSA Administrator Marie Therese Dominguez. "These minimum federal standards will help to prevent incidents like the one at Aliso Canyon from happening in other communities around the country."

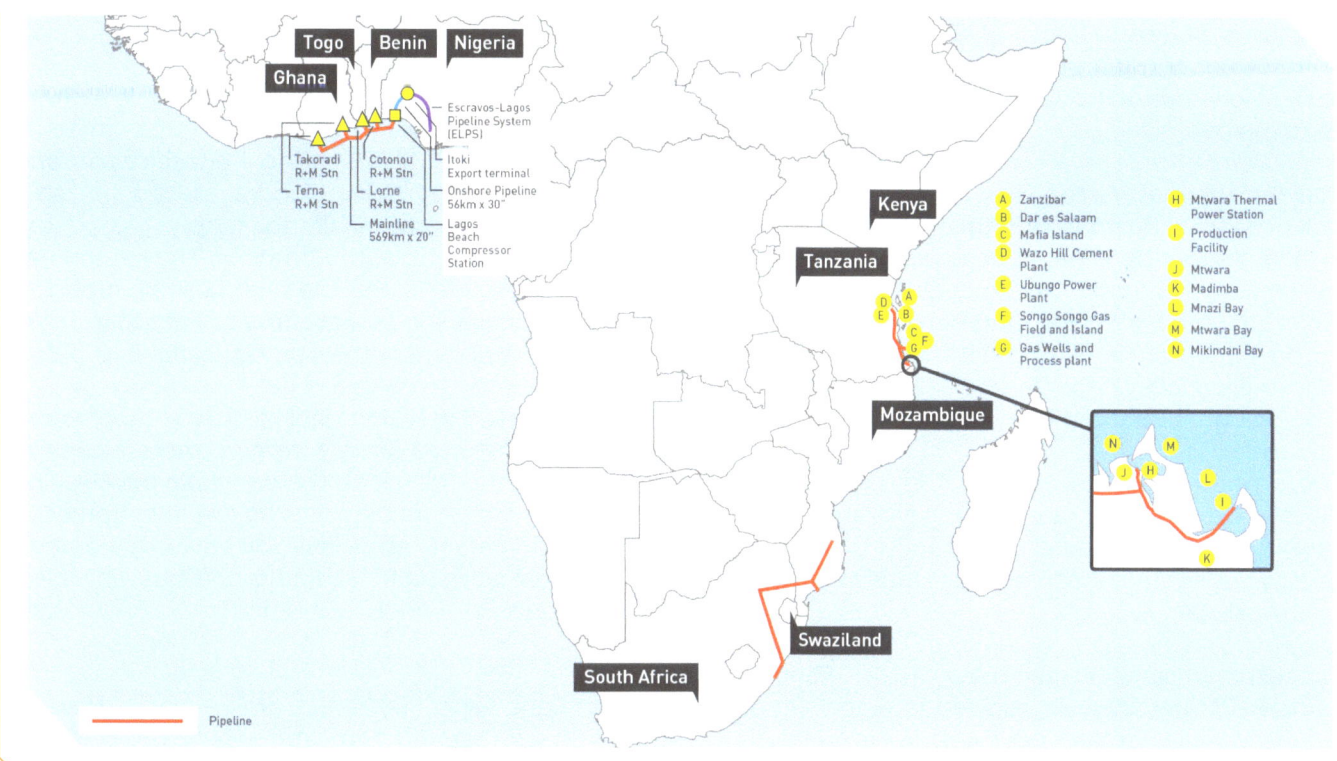

Africa- the Emerging Natural Gas Market Poised to Fuel Growth for African Economies

The recent large offshore natural gas discoveries in Africa have focused the attention of the international oil and gas industry on large LNG export projects that are essential to monetize these resources. Large offshore resources are expensive to develop and projects may not be able to clear investment hurdles if dedicated solely to the domestic gas market.

Developing an LNG export project, however, and reserving a portion of the gas production for the domestic market - with the full support of the host government - can make natural gas available for local use in addition to earning revenue through export. This can enable the development of a diverse market for gas including power generation, local and regional industrial and commercial enterprises, transport, feedstock for petrochemical manufacturing, and other domestic uses of gas for the local population. LNG imports could also enable the development of domestic gas markets throughout Africa.

New Gas Discoveries in Mozambique and Tanzania

More countries in Sub-Saharan Africa are on the cusp of emerging as major natural gas producers. Mozambique and Tanzania recently have discovered more than 250 trillion cubic feet TCF of gas reserves.

In Mozambique, more than 200 TCF of natural gas has been discovered offshore in the Rovuma Basin, while in Tanzania more than 57 TCF of natural gas has been discovered offshore. These giant gas reserves can be a game-changer for the southern African region.

Because the reserves are so large, it is possible to have a good balance between the export of LNG, which will generate needed foreign exchange, and the expansion of the domestic natural gas market to meet the power needs in the country and region, as well as an opportunity to develop local industry. Many downstream projects were presented to Mozambique pursuant to the Mozambique Gas Master Plan, supporting a potential for 26 TCF consumption of natural gas in Mozambique.

The energy demand in the southern Africa countries has increased exponentially each year. In Mozambique, the demand for electricity is

January 2017 • Issue 1

estimated at more than 1,000 megawatts MW in 2016 and may triple in the next 15 years, according to the Mozambican power company, Electricidade de Mocambique EDM.

Besides the gas needed for power, various other downstream industries that utilize gas as feedstock in the production of value-added products are demanding natural gas to produce fertilizers, gas-to-liquid fuels, and methanol, among other products, which may contribute significantly to the industrialization of those countries and associated job creation if they can be made profitable.

The governments and communities expect that the discoveries of natural gas, either in Mozambique or in Tanzania, can contribute significantly to solving the energy crisis in the region, and facilitating investments in downstream projects.

The experience of Mozambique in the Pande and Temane Project – which allowed interconnection of the Pande and Temane gas fields in Mozambique to Secunda, in South Africa, and enabled development of small gas markets within Mozambique - can be quite useful in the Rovuma projects in Mozambique, and Tanzania.

Nigeria and Angola are also important gas producers. The huge shortfall in power supply in Africa, coupled with the relatively high cost of electricity based on the high cost of available fuel in many African countries, presents a new opportunity for natural gas and LNG imports to fuel the projected growth of African economies.

In September 2016, the US Power Africa Roadmap report outlined a goal to increase power generation in sub-Saharan Africa by more than 30,000 megawatts MW by 2030. This translates to about 5.5 bcfd of additional natural gas consumption or about 42 MTPA of LNG, assuming natural gas is the fuel of choice. This is equivalent to the growth of LNG observed in China and India during a similar timeframe. Similarly, the African Development Bank Group has set an aspirational vision to achieve universal access to electricity by 2025. This vision is encapsulated in the New Deal on Energy for Africa.

The domestic natural gas prices in many African countries are quite competitive. The prices are mostly established by bilateral negotiation between buyers and sellers and are usually indexed on alternative fuels such as crude oil or petroleum products, as in the case in Ghana, Mozambique, and Nigeria. The natural gas prices range from about $1.21/MMBtu in Mozambique for industrial customers to around $8.4/MMBtu for power generation in Ghana, with gas

prices in Nigeria falling within the range.

The emerging African natural gas markets will attract pipeline gas and LNG in the near-to-medium term. For example, the LNG Floating Regasification and Storage Unit FSRU Golar Tundra arrived in Tema port in Ghana in July 2016 to supply gas to the Ghana National Petroleum Company. The natural gas price levels in Ghana and the high cost of imported alternative fuel are adequate to accommodate LNG imports to complement the other gas supply sources.

Nigeria delayed development of LNG liquefaction projects after NLNG Train 6 to give more attention to delivering natural gas to the domestic market. The Nigerian government is focusing on the domestic natural gas market, especially for power generation and gas-based industries. Cameroon has one LNG export terminal under construction with another planned.

Mozambique and Tanzania are already making provision for meeting domestic natural gas demand as the terms of the LNG export project are being negotiated. Equatorial Guinea is also one of the LNG exporting nations from sub-Saharan Africa.

Examples of Domestic Gas Projects

Power projects

Gas-to-liquids projects

Fertilizer plans

Petrochemicals

Methanol projects

Gas transmission and distribution pipelines

Fuel for industry such as iron, steel and cement projects

The Three Main Global Gas Markets

Currently, there are three main global gas markets: the Asia-Pacific region, the European region, and the North American/Atlantic Basin region which includes North America, South America, and Latin America. The Asia Pacific region has historically been the largest market for LNG. Japan is the world's largest LNG importer, followed by South Korea and Taiwan. China and India have recently emerged as LNG importers and could become significant buyers of LNG over time.

The growth of LNG in Europe has been more gradual than that in the Asia-Pacific, primarily because

January 2017 • Issue 1

LNG has had to compete with pipeline gas, both domestically produced and imported from Russia. The traditional European importing countries include the UK, France, Spain, Italy, Belgium, Turkey, Greece and Portugal. More recently, a growing number of European countries have constructed LNG import terminals, including Poland, Lithuania, and Croatia.

In North America, the United States, Canada and Mexico have strong pipeline connections and abundant supplies of natural gas. Historically, this region had been able to supply all its natural gas requirements from indigenous supplies. During the supply-constrained 1970s, however, the US began importing LNG from Algeria and four LNG import terminals were built between 1971-1980. The 1980s was a period of oversupply and US LNG import terminals were either mothballed or underutilized.

In the late 1990s, the United States was forecasting a shortage of natural gas, which led to the reactivation of the mothballed terminals and the building of additional import terminals, including Cheniere Energy's Sabine Pass. But by 2010, it became apparent that the US would be a major shale gas producer, making LNG imports unnecessary. The

cargoes that were to be sold in the US were then available to be sold on global markets. Many of the existing US import terminals were subsequently re-designed as LNG liquefaction and export terminals.

In February 2016, Cheniere Energy's Train 1 came online, thus heralding in a new wave of LNG supply. As of early October 2016, DOE had issued final authorizations to export 15.22 billion cubic feet per day Bcf/d of US Lower-48 States domestically sourced natural gas to non-FTA countries.

The following table shows the US large-scale projects have received regulatory approvals and are under construction or operating.

Project	Volume Bcf/d	In Operation
Sabine Pass Cameron, LA	4.14	Feb 2016
Dominion Cove Point Calvert County, MD	0.77	2018
Cameron Cameron, LA	3.53	2018
Freeport Quintana Island, TX	1.8	2018
Corpus Christi Corpus Christi, TX	2.1	2019

January 2017 • Issue 1

Strategic Petroleum Reserve Sales Totaling Nearly 190 Million Barrels to Start in January 2017 Thru 2025

The Department of Energy's DOE Office of Fossil Energy recently announced that it will sell crude oil from the Strategic Petroleum Reserve SPR as early as January 2017. The announcement came after a Continuing Resolution that included a provision for DOE to sell up to $375.4 million in crude oil from the SPR was enacted into law earlier this month. This sale is the first of several planned sales totaling nearly 190 million barrels, Figure 1, during fiscal years 2017 through 2025. These sales reflect provisions in several recent statutes, including sections 403 and 404 of the Bipartisan Budget Act of 2015 BBA, the Fixing America's Surface Transportation Act FAST Act, which became law in December 2015, and the 21st Century Cures Act Cures Act, which became law earlier this month.

As the largest stockpile of government-owned emergency crude oil in the world, the SPR was established to help alleviate significant disruptions in oil supplies from events such as major geopolitical events affecting oil supply, severe weather, and unplanned production, transport, and delivery outages. Located in four storage sites along the Gulf of Mexico, the SPR holds more than 695 million barrels of crude oil as of December 16, or about 97% of its 713.5 million-barrel design capacity.

The following sales have been approved by Congress:

- Section 404 of the BBA included authorization for funding an SPR modernization program to support improvements deemed necessary to preserve the long-term integrity and utility of SPR's infrastructure by selling up to $2 billion worth of SPR crude oil in fiscal years 2017 through 2020. As part

of the BBA, DOE was required to complete a long-term strategic review of the SPR to ensure it meets current and future energy and economic security goals and objectives. The review was issued in September 2016.

- The Section 404 sales volumes are based on an assumption of $50 per barrel. However, the actual final sales volumes will depend on how SPR decides to allocate the sales volumes across those years and the actual price of crude oil at the time of the sales. For the Section 404 sales, SPR must get an appropriation from Congress to approve its requested sales revenue target.

- Section 403 of the BBA mandates SPR crude oil sales for fiscal years 2018 through 2025 on a volumetric basis, rather than on a dollar basis as done in Section 404. The revenues from sales authorized under section 403 will be deposited into the general fund of the U.S. Department of the Treasury.

- The recently passed Cures Act calls for the sale of 25 million barrels of SPR crude oil for fiscal years 2017 through 2019. The first tranche of these sales is expected in late

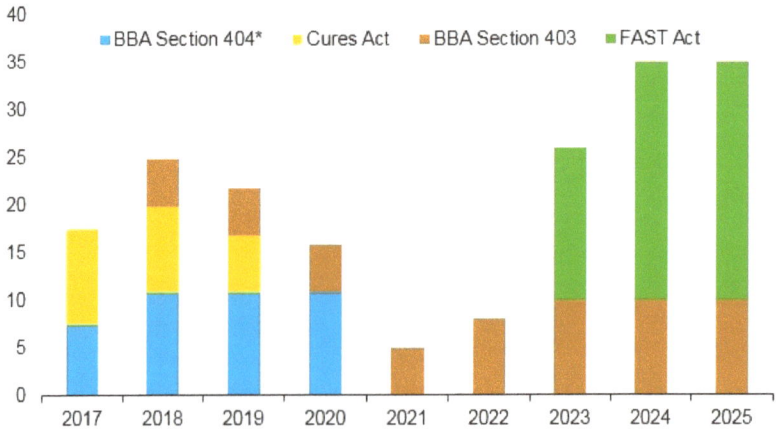

Figure 1. Planned annual Strategic Petroleum Reserve crude oil sales
million barrels

*Note: Volumes sold under the Bipartisan Budget Act of 2015 Section 404 are estimates based on an assumption of $50/barrel.
Source: Strategic Petroleum Reserve.

spring 2017.

- The FAST Act calls for SPR sales totaling 66 million barrels from fiscal years 2023 through 2025.

- As a member of the International Energy Agency IEA, the United States is obligated to maintain stocks of crude oil and petroleum products, both public and private, to provide at least 90 days of net import protection and to collectively participate in the release or sale of oil supplies to help balance a global shortage in the event of a severe energy supply disruption.

- Based on September 2016 levels of net crude oil and petroleum product imports, the SPR alone holds crude oil stocks equivalent to 141 days of import protection.

- The United States must be able to contribute to an IEA collective action based on its share of IEA oil consumption. This obligation can be met by any measure a member nation may choose, including release of strategic or commercial stocks or demand restraint. As of October 2015, the United States must be prepared to contribute 43.9% of the barrels released in an IEA coordinated response. The U.S. government relies on the use of the SPR to meet this requirement.

Shale natural gas proved reserves, reserves changes, and production, 2015 (billion cubic feet)

Changes in Reserves During 2015

	Published		Revision	Revision				New Field	New Reservoir Discoveries	Estimated	Proved
	Proved		Increases	Decreases	Sales	Acquisitions	Extensions	Discoveries	in Old Fields	Production	Reserves
	Reserves	Adjustments									
State and Subdivision	12/31/14	(+,-)	(+)	(-)	(-)	(+)	(+)	(+)	(+)	(-)	12/31/15
Alaska	0	0	0	0	0	0	0	0	0	0	0
Lower 48 States	199,684	12,222	22,271	68,460	7,250	6,461	24,309	0	1,577	15,213	175,601
Arkansas	11,695	17	30	3,890	3	0	238	0	0	923	7,164
California	44	-1	0	10	0	0	0	0	0	2	31
Coastal Region Onshore	9	0	0	0	0	0	0	0	0	1	8
San Joaquin Basin Onshore	15	0	0	2	0	0	0	0	0	1	12
State Offshore	20	-1	0	8	0	0	0	0	0	0	11
Colorado	3,775	288	71	732	0	0	38	0	0	325	3,115
Kansas	4	1	2	1	0	0	0	0	0	1	5
Kentucky	50	-35	0	1	0	0	0	0	0	1	13
Louisiana	12,792	1,351	1,335	4,881	1,212	5	917	0	0	1,153	9,154
North	12,611	1,339	1,307	4,865	1,206	5	910	0	0	1,129	8,972
South	181	12	28	16	6	0	7	0	0	24	182
Michigan	1,432	-283	120	198	0	0	0	0	0	65	1,006
Mississippi	19	2	3	10	0	0	0	0	0	3	11
Montana	482	-31	31	86	0	0	3	0	0	39	360
New Mexico	646	259	54	487	0	35	582	0	1	46	1,044
East	604	268	32	478	0	35	520	0	1	44	938
West	42	-9	22	9	0	0	62	0	0	2	106
North Dakota	6,442	393	1,258	1,267	171	12	776	0	6	545	6,904

Ohio	6,384	1,324	2,412	1,560	1,495	1,409	3,361	0	1,554	959	12,430
Oklahoma	16,653	2,455	2,041	4,527	702	1,332	2,413	0	0	993	18,672
Pennsylvania	56,210	4,017	10,908	22,034	320	0	9,286	0	14	4,597	53,484
Texas	54,158	920	3,431	15,084	2,428	2,868	3,114	0	0	4,353	42,626
RRC District 1	11,729	150	1,195	2,057	423	372	429	0	0	892	10,503
RRC District 2 Onshore	6,648	-187	719	2,730	7	0	795	0	0	793	4,445
RRC District 3 Onshore	106	53	24	53	6	0	18	0	0	17	125
RRC District 4 Onshore	4,991	29	194	1,253	918	939	1,076	0	0	500	4,558
RRC District 5	13,043	829	29	5,034	339	601	2	0	0	903	8,228
RRC District 6	3,979	103	543	1,272	18	22	355	0	0	238	3,474
RRC District 7B	2,204	9	11	753	407	406	2	0	0	143	1,329
RRC District 7C	1,183	-43	300	217	2	8	261	0	0	140	1,350
RRC District 8	1,125	-24	93	552	59	104	158	0	0	109	736
RRC District 8A	10	-3	3	3	0	0	0	0	0	3	4
RRC District 9	9,074	-6	317	1,138	249	416	18	0	0	608	7,824
RRC District 10	66	10	3	22	0	0	0	0	0	7	50
Virginia	84	-3	0	2	65	65	0	0	0	3	76
West Virginia	28,311	1,447	454	13,213	834	735	3,487	0	2	1,163	19,226
Wyoming	380	88	117	419	20	0	94	0	0	36	204
Miscellaneousa	123	13	4	58	0	0	0	0	0	6	76
U.S. Total	199,684	12,222	22,271	68,460	7,250	6,461	24,309	0	1,577	15,213	175,601

[a] Includes Indiana, Missouri, and Tennessee.

BP and Kosmo Energy Partnership to Create a New LNG hub in Africa

BP chief executive officer Bob Dudley said, "BP's entry into Mauritania and Senegal represents an exciting strategic opportunity to work with Kosmos Energy in an emerging world-class hydrocarbon basin. We believe our expertise in integrating the gas value chain, together with a talented exploration partner in Kosmos, along with the support of the Mauritanian and Senegalese governments brings together all the elements needed to **create a new LNG hub in Africa.**"

> **BP's entry into Mauritania and Senegal represents an exciting strategic opportunity to work with Kosmos Energy in an emerging world-class hydrocarbon basin**

exploration blocks in Mauritania and a 32.49 percent effective working interest in Kosmos' Senegal exploration blocks -- acreage which holds world-class deepwater gas discoveries and exploration prospectivity across both countries.

The approximately 33,000 square kilometres of acreage covered by today's agreements includes the Tortue field, estimated by Kosmos to contain more than 15 tcf of discovered gas resources. The total acreage, by Kosmos' estimates, could contain

Following BP signed agreements with Kosmos Energy in which it acquired a 62 percent working interest, including operatorship, of Kosmos' roughly 50tcf of gas resource potential and in excess of 1 billion barrels of liquids resource potential.

January 2017 • Issue 1

BP will invest nearly one billion dollars mostly in the form of a multi-year exploration and development carry to acquire a 62 percent interest and operatorship of offshore Blocks C-6, C-8, C-12 and C-13 in Mauritania and an effective 32.49 percent interest in the Saint-Louis Profond and Cayar Profond blocks in Senegal.

To reduce development time and drive capital efficiency, the partners plan to process and transport the gas from Tortue at a nearshore LNG facility. The proposed complex could be expanded in phases to accommodate future gas discoveries.

Under the terms of the agreements, BP and Kosmos have also agreed that Kosmos will remain the technical operator for the exploration phase of the project and drill three new exploration wells beginning in 2017.

- Under the terms of the agreements, BP will pay Kosmos a cash bonus of $162 million on completion. Moving forward, BP will carry Kosmos' exploration and appraisal costs of $221 million along with Kosmos' development costs of $533 million, including front-end engineering and design studies. Project sanction is expected by 2018.

- Kosmos will also receive a contingent bonus of up to $2 per barrel for up to 1 billion barrels of liquids, as a production royalty, subject to a future liquids discovery and oil price.

- BP's proposed share of the Contractor Group results in a working interest in Mauritania consisting of Société Mauritanienne Des Hydrocarbures et de Patrimoine Minier 10 percent, BP 62 percent and Kosmos 28 percent and an effective working interest in Senegal consisting of Société des Pétroles du Sénégal 10 percent, BP 32.49 percent, Kosmos 32.51 percent and Timis Corporation 25 percent.

In addition to the existing blocks, the companies have agreed to cooperate in areas of mutual interest in offshore Mauritania, Senegal and The Gambia with Kosmos acting as the exploration operator and BP as the development operator.

Subject to government approvals, the agreements are expected to close by the first quarter of 2017.

P O G S March 2017

The Intl Pipeline Oil and GAS Safety Conference and Exhibition

Organized by:

RGT MEDIA COMMUNICATIONS CORP.

March 14-16, 2017 Houston Texas USA

Pipeline Integrity | **Emission Reduction** | **Well Control** | **Oil and Gas Transportation** | **Chemical Extraction**

Connecting Supplier with Procurement Teams

Exhibition

200+
Exhibitors Expected

Attendance

2000+
Attendees Expected

Goal

Improve safety in the entire value chain of the oil and gas industry not limited to the well heads but distribution chains, transportation and supply chain.

Exhibit@ P O G S Safety Tech

P O G S Safety Tech provides international and local energy companies who operate across the up, mid and downstream sectors of the oil &gas supply chain with a B2B platform to meet and influence highly-focused International decision-makers and buyers.

Who is Attending?

Take Advantage of Early Registration- Register Now @

http://www.oilandgassafetyconference.com registration/online-registration/

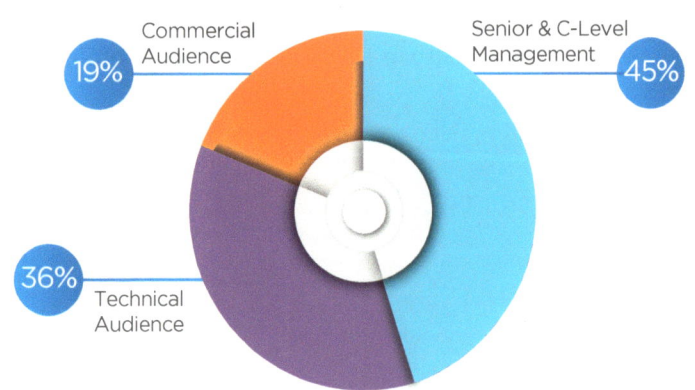

Commercial Audience 19%

Senior & C-Level Management 45%

Technical Audience 36%

Who is Exhibiting?

SHOWFLOOR IS Selling Very Fast RESERVED Today

http://www.oilandgassafetyconference.com/ booth-registeration/

Official Media Partner

USA Oil and Gas Monitor
A RGT Media Communications Corp.

For further details visit website @
http://oilandgassafetyconference.com
or call +1-832-664-0618

The International Pipeline,
Oil and Gas Safety Conference

POGS
Intl Pipeline, Oil and Gas
Safety Conference &
Exhibition

POGS March 14-16, 2017   www.oilandgassafetyconference.com

Goals

This conference seeks to *address process safety issues* in the upstream, midstream and downstream subsectors of the industry; with special focus on well control safety, process safety, pipeline safety, and new regulatory impact.

To help improve operational excellence in the various communities where the industry operates- emerging technologies, leak detection and prevention technologies, emission reduction technologies, compliance audit, best practices to reduce risks and hazards, and improve the overall operational safety is the focal point of this conference.

To help meet these goals - are the speakers and participating companies

Brady Austin
QHSE Service Line Owner Lloyd's Register

Mothusi Pahl
Vice President- Alphabet Energy Inc.

Vincent Higgins
Chairman and CEO Optech4D Inc

Hunter Hawa
Global EHS Director for PSRG

Robert Miller
Regulatory Compliance Specialist, Veriforce

W. Duncan Welder IV
RISC's Director of Client Services

Shoshi Kaganovsky
CEO and founder of SensoLeak

Alexis Vitone
President, AvA Excellence in Business Strategies & HSE, LLC

Tom Meek
Director of Compliance, Veriforce

Keith J. Coyle
Shareholder, Babst Calland

Mark A. Hernandez
President of Multiply Leadership

Rixio Medina
Director of Business Development for the Board of Certified Safety Professionals

Registration Fee - $500

Register Today for this all important industrial conference

Fill out this form email form to: *registration@oilandgassafetyconference.com*

Or mail form with check to the address below.

Mail and make check payable to: *RGT Media Communications Corp.   10777 Westheimer Street, #1100 Houston Texas 77042*

Payment Method -Card type- Amex, Visa, Master, Discovery (circle one)

Card No: _____   Expiration Date: _____   Name on card: _____   By Check Check No: _____

First Name: _____   Last Name: _____

Your Preferred Mailing Address - (Circle One) Business/ Residence

Job Title: _____   Company Name : _____   Street : _____

(No PO Boxes Please) City : _____   State: _____   Country: _____   Zip/Postal Code: ____   cut here

Day Phone: _____   Fax: _____   E-mail: _____

Program Agenda Break Down

Pipeline Safety- Leak Detection and Prevention Tech

Shoshi Kaganovsky - CEO and founder of SensoLeak

Emerging Technologies - Leveraging Virtual and Augmented Reality Technologies for Midstream & pipeline industries

Vincent Higgins - Chairman and CEO Optech4D Inc

Best Practices- Avoiding risks and hazards/ Competency-Based Training Program

Alexis Vitone- President - AvA Excellence in Business Strategies & HSE, LLC

Brady Austin - QHSE Service Line Owner- Lloyd's Register

W. Duncan Welder IV - RISC's Director of Client Services

Motivational Speaker

Mark A. Hernandez - President Multiply Leardership

Process Safety

Hunter Hawa - Global EHS Director for PSRG

PHMSA Regulations

Keith J. Coyle - Shareholder- Attorney at Law - Babst Calland

Emission Reduction Technology- Converting Flares to Power Gen

Mothusi Pahl - Vice President-Alphabet Energy Inc.

Compliance Audit- Federal/State codes and OQ NPRM

Tom Meek - Director of Compliance, Veriforce

Robert Miller - Regulatory Compliance Specialist, Veriforce

Rixio Medina - Director of Business Development for the Board of Certified Safety Professionals

---

Supporting Organization

Pennsylvania Independent Oil and Gas Association
PIOGA

Official Media Partner

USA Oil and Gas Monitor

Member Organization

Independent Petroleum Association of America
IPAA

POGS
Intl Pipeline, Oil and Gas
Safety Conference &
Exhibition

cut here

SOCAR and BP-operated AIOC agrees to Future Development of The Biggest Producing Oil Field in The Caspian Sea

SOCAR the State Oil Company of the Republic of Azerbaijan and AIOC the Azerbaijan International Operating Company signed a letter of intent LoI for the future development of the Azeri-Chirag-Gunashli ACG field in the Azerbaijan sector of the Caspian Sea.

The agreement will cover the development of the field until 2050 and will add significant resource development potential to the middle of the century. Today ACG produces circa 620,000 barrels of oil equivalent.

The shareholders in AIOC are BP, Chevron, INPEX, Statoil, ExxonMobil, TPAO, ITOCHU and ONGC Videsh.

Rovnag Abdullayev commented: "We have been in negotiations with ACG's foreign partners for some time. We will complete fully-termed agreements soon. ACG is known as the "Contract of the Century". It is very important to Azerbaijan - it is the symbol of our oil industry. It has opened a whole new era for the country's development. The Letter of Intent we signed today with ACG's foreign partners signifies that we can now look ahead to many more years of

- Agreement will lead to further significant investment
- Current production from ACG is circa 620,000 barrels of oil equivalent per day
- Will create significant jobs in the years ahead
- BP will lead the partnership

ACG's success."

Bob Dudley, BP CEO, said: "This is an important day for Azerbaijan, SOCAR and the AIOC partnership. It opens an exciting opportunity to the middle of the century for us to continue this extraordinary partnership. In 1994 we set out to develop ACG in the new phase of the country's energy journey. BP is very proud to be a part of this long-term partnership and looks forward to continuing it for many decades to come."

Gordon Birrell added: "As operator of ACG we are

January 2017 • Issue 1

pleased to have the opportunity to continue to lead this world-class field development safely and efficiently. Today's signing allows us to look ahead to the next chapter in ACG's success and indeed in Azerbaijan's energy story. We believe together we will be able to build on this success by continuing to combine the country's potential and experience with leading technology.

"This agreement will enable future investments and projects, and will bring many thousands of jobs in the years ahead."

ACG is a super-giant field located about 100 km east of Baku. It is the biggest producing oil field in the Caspian Sea and covers an area of more than 432 square kilometres. It lies in water depths of between 120 and 170 metres. The depth of the reservoir is 2,000-3,500 metres.

The existing ACG PSA was signed in September 1994 for 30 years. Oil production from the field began in November 1997. To date the field has produced more than 3 billion barrels of oil with around $33 billion of investment.

There are six producing platforms on ACG, linked with a world-class onshore terminal in Sangachal near Baku. From the terminal ACG oil is exported to world markets primarily by the Baku-Tbilisi-Ceyhan oil export pipeline and the Western Route Export Pipeline to Supsa.

BP is the operator acting on behalf of AIOC and the Contractor Parties to the ACG Production Sharing Agreement.

The LoI was signed in Baku by Rovnag Abdullayev, President of SOCAR, on behalf of the Republic of Azerbaijan, and by Gordon Birrell, BP's Regional President for Azerbaijan, Georgia and Turkey, on behalf of the AIOC partnership.

The LoI agrees the key commercial terms for the future development of the ACG field and enables the parties to conclude negotiations and finalize fully-termed agreements in the next few months.

Rex Tillerson to Retire, Darren Woods Elected Chairman, CEO of Exxon Mobil Corporation

Rex W. Tillerson, chairman and chief executive officer of Exxon Mobil Corporation NYSE:XOM, has announced his intention to retire at year-end after more than 41 years of service.

Darren W. Woods, currently president of Exxon Mobil Corporation, has been elected chairman and chief executive officer by the board of directors effective Jan. 1, 2017.

The board of directors congratulated Tillerson on his nomination for the position of U.S. secretary of state.

"We thank Rex for his leadership, service and dedication to ExxonMobil," said the board. He led the company with integrity and honor, ensuring that safety and environmental protection were at the forefront of everything we do, generating value for shareholders and highlighting the impressive accomplishments of the company's diverse workforce throughout the world. We know that his service to the nation as secretary of state will be equally successful and distinguished."

Tillerson was scheduled to retire in March 2017 when he reached 65, the company's mandatory retirement age for his position. After consideration, Tillerson concluded, and the board agreed, that given the significant requirements associated with the confirmation process, it was appropriate to move the retirement date.

Tillerson joined Exxon Company USA in 1975 as a production engineer. He held various senior roles in the corporation throughout his career spanning more than four decades, including executive vice president of ExxonMobil Development Company.

He was named senior vice president of Exxon Mobil Corporation in 2001 and was elected president and member of the board of directors in 2004. Tillerson was elected chairman and chief executive officer in January 2006.

Woods, 51, was elected president of ExxonMobil and a member of the board of directors in January 2016.
Born in Wichita, Kansas, Woods joined Exxon

Company International in 1992. During his career, he held various senior domestic and international positions in ExxonMobil Refining & Supply Company, ExxonMobil Chemical Company and Exxon Company International. He also served as manager of ExxonMobil investor relations.

In 2012, he was appointed president of ExxonMobil Refining & Supply Company and a vice president of the corporation. In this role, Woods had primary responsibility for the company's global refining, supply and transportation activities. In 2014, he was named a senior vice president of the corporation and became a member of its management committee.

Woods earned a bachelor's degree in electrical engineering from Texas A&M University and a master's degree in business administration from Northwestern University's Kellogg School of Management.

Effective and disciplined succession planning is critical to the corporation's ongoing success and a key component of its competitive advantage. This change in leadership is consistent with the board of directors' succession plan developed years in advance and demonstrates the strength of the management development system.

With the retirement of Tillerson, the ExxonMobil board now is comprised of 12 directors, 11 of whom are non-employees.

In the meantime, Tom Walters, president, ExxonMobil Production Company, has announced his intention to retire after more than 38 years of service.

Neil Duffin, currently president of ExxonMobil Development Company, has been appointed by the Exxon Mobil Corporation NYSE:XOM board of directors to be president of ExxonMobil Production Company and elected to be a vice president of the corporation.

Liam Mallon, currently executive vice president of ExxonMobil Development Company, has been elected president of ExxonMobil Development

January 2017 • Issue 1

Company by its board of directors. All changes are effective Jan. 1.

Walters joined Exxon USA in 1978 in Los Angeles and has held a variety of technical and managerial positions in production, operations, development and global services. In 1999, he was appointed vice president for Africa for ExxonMobil Development Company and in 2002, vice president, United States, for ExxonMobil Production Company.

He was appointed president, ExxonMobil Global Services Company in 2005 prior to becoming executive vice president of ExxonMobil Development Company in 2007. He became president of ExxonMobil Gas & Power Marketing Company in 2009 and was appointed to his current role as president of ExxonMobil Production Company in 2013.

Walters was born in Hammond, Indiana, and is a graduate of Vanderbilt University with a bachelor's degree in mechanical engineering and from Texas A&M University with a master's degree in ocean engineering.

Duffin joined Mobil in 1979 in Aberdeen, Scotland, and has held a variety of managerial positions in production, operations and development.

In 1992, he was named producing advisor for Europe and Africa based in Fairfax, Virginia. In 1995, he moved to Aberdeen, Scotland, as operations and northern North Sea manager, and in 1998, he was named senior vice president, Mobil Oil Indonesia, with responsibility for exploration and producing operations throughout the country.

Duffin became vice president, ExxonMobil Development Company for Russia/Caspian Sea and the Middle East in 1999. He became vice president of ExxonMobil Production Company for Africa in 2004. He became executive vice president of ExxonMobil Development Company in 2006 and was elected as president of ExxonMobil Development Company in 2007.

Duffin was born in St. Andrews, Scotland. He is a graduate of Heriot Watt University, Edinburgh, UK, with a bachelor's degree in mechanical engineering.

Mallon joined Mobil in 1990 in Aberdeen, Scotland, and held a variety of progressively senior positions before he became operations manager in Nigeria in 1998. He moved to Australia in the same capacity in 2000, and in 2003 relocated to Houston where he was planning manager for ExxonMobil Production Company.

In 2004, Mallon was appointed president of ExxonMobil Canada, and in 2006 he was appointed director and chairman of ExxonMobil subsidiaries in Malaysia. He was made vice president of engineering for ExxonMobil Production Company in 2009 and vice president for Africa in 2012. He was appointed to his current position as executive vice president of ExxonMobil Development Company in 2014.

Mallon was born in Drogheda, Ireland, and is a graduate of Trinity College in Dublin with a bachelor's degree in mechanical engineering and from Heriot Watt in Edinburgh with a master's in petroleum engineering.

ExxonMobil Announces New Natural Gas Discovery Onshore Papua New Guinea

Exxon Mobil Corporation NYSE:XOM has announced a new natural gas discovery in the Papua New Guinea North Highlands, 13 miles 21 kilometers northwest of the Hides Gas Field. Interest owners are ExxonMobil 42.5 percent, Oil Search Limited 37.5 percent and Barracuda Limited, a subsidiary of Santos Limited 20 percent, subject to regulatory approval, with Oil Search as operator.

The Muruk-1 well encountered similar high-quality sandstone reservoirs as the Hides field and was in line with pre-drill expectations. It was safely drilled to

- Muruk-1 well encounters high-quality hydrocarbon-bearing reservoirs
- Evaluation of the resource underway

10,630 feet 3,130 meters. Evaluation is underway to determine the size of the discovery.

"We are excited by the results of the Muruk-1

exploration well, which confirms the presence of hydrocarbons in the same high-quality sandstone reservoirs as the Hides field that underpins the PNG LNG project," said Steve Greenlee, president of ExxonMobil Exploration Company. "Over the coming months, we will work with our co-venturers to better determine the full resource potential."

"ExxonMobil has been involved in exploration in Papua New Guinea since the 1930s," Greenlee added. "The Muruk exploration success demonstrates the strength of ExxonMobil's long-term investment approach and reaffirms its commitment to Papua New Guinea."

Oil Search began drilling the Muruk-1 well on Nov. 2, 2016.

The well is in petroleum prospecting license 402, which covers 126,000 acres 510 square kilometers.

ExxonMobil's Energy Outlook Projects Population, Economic Growth to Drive Energy Demand

Global population growth of nearly 2 billion, a doubling of worldwide economic output and rapid expansion of the middle class in emerging economies are all expected to contribute to energy demand growth of about 25 percent from 2015 to 2040, according to ExxonMobil's 2017 Outlook for Energy: A View to 2040.

Efficiency gains across economies worldwide will play a significant role in limiting the growth in energy needs. Energy demand in member nations of the Organization for Economic Co-operation and Development OECD is likely to be flat to 2040, while demand in non-OECD nations is expected to increase 40 percent as prosperity expands and access to modern energy increases.

Growth in global energy demand will be led by greater electrification of the global economy. Fifty-five percent of the energy demand growth over the next quarter century will be tied to power generation needed to support the increasingly digital and plugged-in lives of society, according to the Outlook for Energy, the company's annual long-range supply-and-demand energy forecast.

Average electricity use per household will rise about 30 percent between 2015 and 2040. The share of the world's electricity generated by coal is expected to fall to about 30 percent from approximately 40 percent in 2015 as the use of lower-emission energy sources including natural gas, nuclear and renewables increases.

"As economies expand around the world, energy demand will increase as more people seek higher standards of living," said William Colton, vice president of corporate strategic planning of Exxon Mobil Corporation NYSE:XOM. "Humanity's dual challenge is to meet growing energy demand while managing the risk of climate change. Our Outlook for Energy can help people understand factors influencing future energy supply and demand and inform industries and governments as they consider future energy policy."

With the global middle class, more than doubling to about 5 billion, the number of cars, sport-utility

January 2017 • Issue 1

vehicles and pickups are expected to increase about 80 percent to 1.8 billion vehicles by 2040. During the same period, average new car fuel economy will improve from about 30 miles per gallon to nearly 50 miles per gallon, reflecting significant strides in efficiency of conventional vehicles and a shift in the fleet mix favoring hybrid vehicles, the report shows.

Global energy-related carbon dioxide emissions are expected to peak during the 2030s and then gradually decline. This is supported by an increasing shift to less carbon-intensive energy for power generation and higher energy efficiency across all sectors.

The Outlook for Energy is ExxonMobil's long-range forecast developed by its economists, engineers and scientists through data-driven analysis. It examines energy supply and demand trends for approximately 100 countries, 15 demand sectors and 20 different energy types. ExxonMobil uses the forecast as a foundation for its business strategies and to help guide multi-billion-dollar investment decisions.

Key findings of the report include:

- From 2015 to 2040, global demand for energy is expected to increase by about 25 percent – roughly equivalent to the total energy used today in North America and Latin America.

- In 2040, oil and natural gas are expected to make up nearly 60 percent of global supplies, while nuclear and renewables will be approaching 25 percent.

- Natural gas demand will expand significantly, accounting for about 40 percent of the projected growth in global energy demand.

- Nuclear and renewable energy sources – including bio-energy, hydro, geothermal, wind, and solar – are also likely to account for 40 percent of the growth in global energy demand to 2040.

- Oil will provide about one third of the world's energy in 2040, remaining the No. 1 source of fuel, with growth driven by commercial transportation and chemicals demand. Average global fuel economy for new light-duty vehicles is expected to improve by about two-thirds.

- Carbon intensity of the global economy is likely to be reduced by 45 percent through 2040, reflecting significant gains in the energy efficiency of economies worldwide and a gradual transition to lower carbon-intensive energy types.

- Global energy-related carbon dioxide emissions are likely to peak during the 2030s and begin to decline, even as global economic output doubles from 2015 to 2040.

- North America, which for decades had been an oil importer, is likely to become a significant net exporter by 2025.

- India is likely to surpass China as the world's most populous nation by 2025. The two countries are expected to account for about 45 percent of the growth in global energy demand.

Clay Neff Named President of Chevron Africa and Latin America Exploration and Production

Chevron Corporation NYSE:CVX has named Clay Neff president of Chevron Africa and Latin America Exploration and Production, effective January 1, 2017.

Neff, 54, succeeds Ali Moshiri, who will retire from Chevron after 38 years of distinguished service, effective April 1, 2017, consistent with the company's mandatory retirement policy. Neff, who is currently managing director of Chevron's Nigeria Mid-Africa Business Unit, will oversee Chevron's exploration and production activities in 15 countries across Africa and Latin America. In his new role, Neff will report to Jay Johnson, Chevron's executive vice president, Upstream.

In his current role, Neff is responsible for Chevron's upstream operations in Nigeria and West Africa. He received his Bachelor's degree in Petroleum Engineering from Louisiana State University in 1984 and joined Chevron the following year as a drilling engineer. Since then, he has held numerous engineering, operations, commercial and management positions of increasing responsibility in the United States, Angola and Nigeria. Mr. Neff is also the chairman of the board of trustees for the Foundation for Partnership Initiatives in the Niger Delta PIND, chairman of the Oil Producers Trade Section of the Lagos Chamber of Commerce & Industry, and a member of the Society of Petroleum Engineers.

Over the course of his career, Moshiri has developed significant operational and international experience. He has held key leadership roles throughout the enterprise, including manager of Petroleum and Facilities Engineering, general manager of Strategic Planning and Assets Evaluation for Chevron Overseas Petroleum, general manager and advisor to the vice chairman of the board of Chevron Corporation Exploration and Production, and managing director of Chevron Latin America Exploration and Production Company.

"Clay's broad operating experience, particularly in Africa, makes him highly qualified to lead these two key regions for our business," said John Watson, Chevron's chairman and CEO.

Commenting on Moshiri's retirement, Watson said, "Ali has played a central and critical role in growing our business in Africa and Latin America. He has also distinguished himself as a champion of Chevron's commitment to economic and social development in the areas in which we operate."

Chevron Announces Sale of Geothermal Operations-Assets in Indonesia and the Philippines

Chevron Corporation NYSE:CVX has announced that its wholly-owned subsidiaries have entered into a sales and purchase agreement with Star Energy Consortium to sell Chevron's Indonesian and Philippines Geothermal assets.

"These assets deliver reliable energy to support the needs of Asia-Pacific's growing economies," said Jay Johnson, executive vice president, Upstream, Chevron Corporation. "This sale is aligned with our strategy to maximize the value of our global upstream businesses through effective portfolio management."

In Indonesia, Chevron subsidiaries operate the Darajat and Salak geothermal fields in West Java. In the Philippines, company subsidiaries have a 40 percent equity interest in the Philippine Geothermal Production Company, Inc., which operates the Tiwi and Mak-Ban geothermal power plants in Southern Luzon.

January 2017 • Issue 1

BP and Woolworths Partnership Will Deliver a World-Class Fuel and Convenience Offer for Australian Consumers

BP and Woolworths Group has announced that they have agreed to enter a strategic partnership that will include BP acquiring, rebranding and operating Woolworths' existing 527 fuel and convenience sites across Australia, as well as an additional 16 sites currently under construction, for a total consideration of US$1.3 billion.

The partnership is an exciting prospect for Australian customers with BP and Woolworths set to deliver a fuel and convenience store and loyalty offer unlike any other in Australia. Key features of the offer are:

- Reinventing convenience with a truly differentiated offer, to be branded Metro at BP, that includes a strong seasonal selection of high quality, ready-to-eat and take home fresh food products.

- It is proposed that BP will become a cornerstone partner in Woolworths' Everyday Rewards loyalty program, inviting customers to earn rewards points on both fuel and in-store purchases at any BP site in Australia.

- For the first time, Woolworths' Everyday Rewards cardholders would also be able to redeem points at the register as discounts on purchases at BP.

- BP will maintain the Woolworths' 4 cents per liter redemption offer in the 527 fuel and convenience sites acquired from Woolworths, and will expand this

offer to additional BP sites, giving customers even more reasons to enjoy BP's quality fuels.

Tufan Erginbilgic, Chief Executive, BP Downstream, commented, "The development of high-quality, differentiated fuel and convenience offers is a key part of BP's strategy – allowing us to grow our marketing business in important global markets. We are excited to be establishing this strategic partnership with Woolworths, one of Australia's largest supermarket retailers. Globally we have developed a winning retail formula where we partner with strong local brands, like Marks & Spencer in the UK, to provide our customers with a convenience retail offer that meets the needs of their busy lifestyles. The combination of all aspects of this strategic partnership is expected to create significant value for BP."

Initially, BP and Woolworths will launch a Metro at BP pilot program across 16 BP fuel and convenience sites, allowing both companies to test the offer and generate customer feedback. A second phase will see a further expansion of the Metro at BP format across more than 200 sites.

Andy Holmes, President BP Australia, added, "Over the past three years BP has significantly invested in its fuel and convenience sites across Australia. The opportunity to grow our retail business and work alongside Woolworths, with their strength in grocery and food innovation, will

January 2017 • Issue 1

further enhance our customers' fuel and convenience retail experience. We enjoy strong, successful commercial partnerships with our many dealers, distributors and suppliers and we look forward to sharing the benefits this transaction brings to us all. While Woolworths fuel business has solid foundations, the future combination of BP's international experience and expertise in fuel and convenience offers with Woolworths high quality food products and loyalty program means that BP expects to realize significant improvements in value."

The acquisition of Woolworths' fuel and convenience sites will add to BP's existing network of 350 company-owned retail sites across Australia. BP also supplies fuel and branding to a further 1,000 sites owned by independent business partners.

Brad Banducci, Woolworths Group Chief Executive Officer, said, "For Woolworths customers our Strategic Partnership with BP will enable them to enjoy our leading Woolworths Reward program at BP fuel sites and ensure they continue to benefit from the 4cpl fuel discount. Longer term, it will also provide them with a compelling, new "food-on-the go" offering through the roll-out of the "Metro at BP" concept."

The transaction, which is subject to approval from the Australian Competition and Consumer Commission ACCC and the Foreign Investment Review Board (FIRB), is expected to complete over the next 12 months.

BP in Australia

- There are currently 1,400 BP branded fuel and convenience retail sites across Australia, of which 350 are company-owned. The rest are branded BP but owned by independent business partners.

- BP is one of the largest suppliers of fuel to Australia's industrial and commercial sectors.

- BP is one of Australia's most significant investors, most visibly through our terminals, retail fuel sites and refinery, as founding participants in the North-West Shelf and Browse joint ventures and operator of exploration permits in the Carnarvon Basin. We continue to invest in local economies, growing jobs and building infrastructure in metropolitan and regional Australia.

- BP is engaged in the exploration and production of oil, natural gas and liquefied natural gas and the refining and marketing of petroleum and lubricant products.

Woolworths in Australia

- Founded in 1924, Woolworths Group is Australia's largest retailer with more than 3,500 stores across Australia and New Zealand that span food, drinks, petrol, general merchandise and hotels.

- BP will be establishing a strategic partnership with Woolworths, one of Australia's largest supermarket retailers. The agreement includes BP acquiring, rebranding and operating Woolworths' existing 527 fuel and convenience sites, as well as an additional 16 sites currently under construction, across Australia for a total consideration of US$1.3 billion.

- A new fuel and convenience offer, Metro at BP, will be the first of its kind for Australia's growing convenience sector, bringing together BP's quality fuels, Woolworths' Everyday Rewards, fuel discount dockets and a new range of high-quality, ready-to-eat and take home fresh food products.

- The combination of BP's international experience and expertise in fuel and convenience offers, with Woolworths' network, high-quality food products and loyalty program is an exciting prospect for customers and is expected to create additional value for BP.

- Initially, the partners will launch a Metro at BP pilot program across 16 BP fuel and convenience sites and phase two of the program will expand the Metro at BP format across more than 200 sites.

- BP's global expertise and experience has delivered leading fuel and convenience offers through major partnerships around the world, including with Marks & Spencer in the UK and REWE in Germany.

- The transaction will be subject to Australian Competition and Consumer Commission ACCC and Foreign Investment Review Board FIRB approval.

- Woolworths Group manages some of Australia's most recognized and trusted brands - including Woolworths, Countdown, Dan Murphy's, BWS and BIG W - and endeavors to create a world class experience for customers across all its stores and platforms.

- In FY'16, Woolworths Group generated more than $58 billion in revenue.

- The Woolworths Group is a proud, home-grown Australian business, an employer of more than 205,000 people, and a committed business partner of many thousands of local farmers, producers and manufacturers.

January 2017 • Issue 1

In 2017: Clean Natural Gas Powered Electricity Is Coming to A Plug Near You

The Stonewall power plant in Loudoun County, Virginia, represents another step in the power industry's march towards natural gas and away from coal – a transition that has reshaped how Americans get electricity.

The 778 megawatt natural gas-fired power plant on the outskirts of Washington D.C. is scheduled to go live in 2017 and is expected to generate electricity for nearly 780,000 homes. The facility is owned by Panda Power Funds, a Dallas, Texas-based energy investor.

Stonewall is just one of several natural gas-fired power plants slated to go live next year. The Energy Information Agency is predicting that 2016 will be the first year that natural gas-fired generation exceeds coal generation in the United States on an annual basis when roughly 34 percent of electric power

generation is expected to come from natural gas, and 30 percent from coal.

Stonewall is just one of several natural gas-fired power projects transforming the power sector in the U.S. and beyond. In New York State, Stonewall owner Panda Power Funds is transitioning the Greenidge Generation facility from a coal-fired to natural gas-fired plant. The trend also extends beyond the U.S. In its latest Outlook for Energy report, ExxonMobil projects that by 2040, 25 percent of global energy demand will be met by natural gas.

Several factors are spurring the switch to natural gas. First, the fuel is less carbon-intensive, emitting up to 60 percent less CO_2 than coal when used in power generation, which will help reduce emissions. This has been the case in the United States, where emissions are

at the lowest levels since the 1990s. The fuel is also versatile. It is not only a reliable source of electricity, but also increasingly used in transportation. While many people think of buses when they think of natural gas vehicles, by 2040 liquefied natural gas is expected to meet about 30 percent of the U.S. freight rail industry's energy needs.

This ongoing transformation of the domestic energy landscape has not just added new options to the country's portfolio of energy sources, but it has also generated economic gains in the form of jobs associated with natural gas production, power plant construction and the boost in manufacturing from lower energy costs.

Shell Agrees Sale of Stake In Vivo Energy to Vitol Africa BV

Shell has signed an agreement with Vitol Africa B.V. to sell its 20 per cent shareholding in Vivo Energy for US$250 million. Completion of this transaction is expected during the first half of 2017, subject to regulatory approval.

The sale is in line with Shell's strategy to concentrate its Downstream operations where it can be most competitive.

As part of the transaction, a long-term brand license agreement has been renewed with Vitol to ensure that the Shell brand will remain visible in more than 16 countries across Africa.
About Vivo Energy

Vivo Energy, the Shell licensee in 16 African markets, was established on 1st December 2011 to distribute and market Shell-branded fuels and lubricants. Vivo Energy provides high quality solutions for motorists and businesses in Botswana, Burkina Faso, Cape Verde, Ghana, Guinea, Ivory Coast, Kenya, Mali, Mauritius, Madagascar, Morocco, Mozambique, Namibia, Senegal, Tunisia and Uganda. Its retail offering includes fuels, lubricants, card services, shops and other non-fuel services e.g. oil change and car wash.

For businesses, it provides fuels, lubricants and liquefied petroleum gas LPG to business customers across a range of sectors including marine, mining, and manufacturing. Jet fuel is sold to customers at 23 airports though a partnership with Vitol Aviation. The company employs around 2,300 people, operates over 1,700 retail service stations under the Shell brand and has access to approximately 900,000 cubic metres of fuel storage capacity.

Shell and Vivo Lubricants has blending capacity of around 124,000 metric tons at plants in six countries, Ghana, Guinea, Ivory Coast, Kenya, Morocco, and Tunisia producing Shell branded lubricants.

SHELL Completes the Sale of Shell Refining Company in Malaysia

Shell has completed the sale of its 51per cent shareholding in the Shell Refining Company Federation of Malaya Berhad SRC in Malaysia, which includes the 125,000 barrel per day refinery in Port Dickson, to Malaysia Hengyuan International Limited MHIL for $66.3 million.

Shell is the leading retail fuels and lubricants provider in Malaysia, which remains an important market for the company. Shell will maintain supply to its retail and commercial customers, and will honor all current commercial arrangements through existing comprehensive supply agreements in the country.

This divestment is consistent with Shell's strategy to concentrate its global downstream operations in areas where it can be most competitive.

January 2017 • Issue 1

Shell Completes the Sale of Its Shareholding in Showa Shell to Idemitsu

Shell has completed the sale of a 31.2 per cent shareholding in Showa Shell Sekiyu K.K. to Idemitsu Kosan Co. Ltd. for a total amount of JPY159 billion approximately US$1.4 billion. Completion follows anti-trust approval from the Japan Fair Trade Commission.

John Abbott, Shell Downstream Director, said: "Shell has enjoyed a long and valuable partnership with Showa Shell since the year 1900. I would like to thank CEO Tsuyoshi Kameoka, the management and the board of directors for their leadership and support, as well as those leaders who have preceded them over the last century. I wish the company success and look forward to seeing the commercial linkages and a new relationship between our two companies over the coming years."

The sale supports Shell's strategic commitment to focus downstream activity on areas where it can be most competitive.

Shell's upstream, integrated gas, chemicals and trading businesses are not impacted by the sale. Japan remains an important LNG market for Shell.

IntelliRed™ software: Catching fugitive emissions

The wicked-smart algorithm that can see and subtract

When operating large and complex gas-processing facilities, it is critical that energy professionals maintain a safe and environmentally responsible workplace by detecting and mitigating hydrocarbon leaks. That's why ExxonMobil developed IntelliRed, a sophisticated computer algorithm integrated with an infrared-based optical gas imager that provides a highly sensitive and accurate early warning of leaks.

So how does it work?
Traditionally, operators used handheld optical gas imagers to find leaks. But that method required them to be near the leak, which meant intermittent monitoring—it also had the potential of putting them at risk. The challenge, therefore, was to figure out how to automate the technology so it continuously monitored a facility for potential leaks, removing the operator from the vicinity and improving the efficiency of leak detection.

IntelliRed uses two infrared cameras that are slightly offset from each other: one tracks the background signature in each field of view, and the other captures and processes both hydrocarbons and the background signature. The algorithm analyzes the images captured by the lenses and subtracts the background image, making it easier to zero in on a potential leak. This is a continuous process, so that when there is an actual hydrocarbon leak, it takes far less time to find and stop it.

That ensures safety of the operation and reduces the potential for leaks of methane, which is a powerful greenhouse gas.

OPEC Assumes Its Traditional Role to Stabilize World Oil Market

Production Cut By 1.2 Mb/D in Effect

Following the 'Vienna Agreement' decided upon at the 171st Meeting of the Conference of the Organization of the Petroleum Exporting Countries OPEC on 30th November, 2016, Ministers from OPEC met with several Ministers from non-OPEC oil producing countries on Saturday, 10th December, at the OPEC Secretariat in Vienna, to reassure the world that OPEC still plays an important stabilizing role in the world oil markets.

OPEC Secretary General, HE Mohammad Sanusi Barkindo, during his recent visit to the United States said, "In the last few years, there has been talk that perhaps OPEC was no longer important and that it had possibly lost the key role it has played in the world of energy since its founding," he said. "Well, ladies and gentlemen, I am here to report to you that OPEC is alive and well. Any naysayers that may have had doubts about OPEC's efficacy were proven wrong with the historic decisions made in Vienna at the last OPEC Ministerial Conference on 30

November and between OPEC and non-OPEC countries on 10 December."

The OPEC and non-OPEC Ministerial Meeting held in Vienna December 10,2016 agreed to the following:

- OPEC maintains its decision made on 30th November 2016, whereby arrangements were recorded following the extensive understanding of OPEC's adjustment;

- Azerbaijan, Kingdom of Bahrain, Brunei Darussalam, Equatorial Guinea, Kazakhstan, Malaysia, Mexico, Sultanate of Oman, the Russian Federation, Republic of Sudan, and Republic of South Sudan commit to reduce their respective oil production, voluntarily or through managed decline, in accordance with an accelerated schedule. The combined reduction target was agreed at 558,000 barrels a day for the producers;

- That two participating non-OPEC countries shall join the

OPEC Ministerial Monitoring Committee, consisting of oil ministers, chaired by Kuwait with the Russian Federation as alternate chair and assisted by the OPEC Secretariat;

- To strengthen their cooperation, including through joint analyses and outlooks, with a view to ensuring a sustainable oil market, for the benefit of producers and consumers; and

- To regularly review at the technical and ministerial levels the status of their cooperation.

OPEC Member Countries met on 30th November 2016 and decided to implement a production adjustment of 1.2 million barrels a day mb/d, effective from 1st January 2017. The Meeting recorded that OPEC Member Countries, in agreeing to this decision, confirmed their commitment to a stable and balanced oil market and underscored the importance of other oil producing countries joining their efforts.